FAIRVIEW SCHOOL

SCIENCE IN ANCIENT CHINA

GEORGE BESHORE

SCIENCE IN ANCIENT CHINA

Franklin Watts
New York   London   Toronto   Sydney
A First Book

Library of Congress Cataloging-in-Publication Data

Beshore, George
Science in ancient China / George Beshore.

p.   cm. — (A First book)

Bibliography: p.
Includes index.
Summary: Surveys the achievements of the ancient Chinese in
science, medicine, astronomy, and cosmology, and describes such
innovations as rockets, wells, the compass, water wheels, and
movable type.
ISBN 0-531-10485-0
1. Science—China—History—Juvenile literature.   2. Engineering—
China—History—Juvenile literature.   3. Science, Ancient—Juvenile
literature.   [1. Science—China—History.   2. Technology—China—
History.   3. Inventions—China—History.   4. Science, Ancient.]
I. Title.
Q127.C5B475   1988
509.51—dc 19   87-23748   CIP   AC

To Margaret

CONTENTS

SCIENCE IN
ANCIENT CHINA

Marco Polo, the Venetian explorer who
traveled in China in the thirteenth century

1

TO THE EAST, A DIFFERENT WORLD

When the European traveler Marco Polo visited China in 1275, he was amazed at the technical wonders he found in that foreign land. People shot rockets into the air, printed books with pieces of type that could be used over and over, and found their way across trackless seas with a strange instrument containing a needle that always pointed in the same direction.

No one in Europe had heard of these inventions. Nor did they know how to weave silk into fine fabrics as the Chinese did, or how to heat water by burning the black, rocklike substance, coal. In the countryside the Chinese people had built paved highways connecting great walled cities that had wide, straight streets. Everywhere Marco Polo went, he found evidence of a civilization far more technologically advanced than his native Italy.

The wonders he saw all about him were the result of centuries of scientific advances in astronomy, mathematics, and physics. The Chinese people had been using science and technology since ancient times to improve their way of life.

Technology refers to humankind's application of science to the things people use from day to day. *Science*, then as now, refers to people's search for knowledge about the natural world they live in.

In ancient times this search was done much differently from the way it is done today. People tried to reason about the way they thought things should work in nature instead of performing experiments, as scientists do today. The ancient Chinese excelled in the search for scientific truths as well as in the application of what they had learned to their daily lives.

Great contrasts between science in ancient China and that in the Western world developed because towering mountains and harsh deserts separated the cities of the East from those in the West. These obstacles made travel between China and Europe almost impossible. For this reason one of the world's oldest civilizations developed in relative isolation.

The ancient beginnings of China have been shrouded by time. Modern scientists have found evidence that early humans roamed the area of northern China over 500,000 years ago. Civilization developed slowly. Stone tools found in ancient sites reveal the beginnings of a culture in the river valleys of Eastern Asia over seven thousand years ago.

Ancient Chinese legends say that early rulers taught the people how to raise food and govern themselves some five thousand years ago. This was about the same time the Egyptians were building the Great Pyramid in the Valley of the Nile. The same Chinese legends also claim that other mythical rulers showed their people how to domesticate animals, raise silkworms, and farm the land during the next several hundred years.

THE POWER OF CULTURE

A system of writing was needed to record the results of scientific work as well as the practical application of science. Chinese writing goes back more than 3,500 years. At that time, more than a century before Moses led the people of Israel out of Egypt, the Chinese scratched short messages on animal bones. The writing

ANCIENT CHINA
~ 1275 A.D.

PERSIA

CASPIAN SEA

ARAL SEA

Amu Darya River (Oxus)

AFGHANISTAN

SILK ROAD

INDIA

HIMALAYAN MTS.

ALTAI MTS.

MONGOLIA

GOBI DESERT

Tun-Huang

Sinkiang (Xinjiang)

KUNLUN MTS.

Tibet (Xizana)

CHINA

GREATER KHINGAN MTS.

Manchuria (Dongbei)

GREAT WALL

Peking (Beijing)

Grand Canal

(Huang Ho)

Yellow River

Chungking (Chongqing)

Yangtze River (Changjiang)

Wuhan

Hunan

Canton (Guangzhou)

Shantung (Shandong)

Shanghai

Nanking (Nanjing)

KOREA

JAPAN

PACIFIC OCEAN

they used was ancestral to that found in China today; this makes Chinese the oldest written language continuously used anywhere in the world.

Like other civilizations, China traces its beginnings to the rich river valleys, where farmers could produce extra food. This freed part of the population to build cities, to write books, and to develop the nation's art, music, and science.

Unlike the early peoples who settled in the Nile and the Tigris-Euphrates valleys of the Middle East, the Chinese did not remain within these narrow limits. Rather, they spread their influence across a vast area. Long before the birth of Christ, the Chinese ruled an area larger than the eastern half of the United States. Today, China is the third largest country in the world, after the Soviet Union and Canada. It covers an area of nearly 4 million square miles (10 million sq km).

In order to control this vast area, the early emperors linked their cities by means of paved roads, cutting through mountain passes and building bridges over rushing rivers. Over three thousand years ago the Chinese rulers were sending out orders and getting back regular reports from frontier areas more than a thousand miles (over 1,500 km) from their capital city. Such communications were unheard of in Europe at the time.

FIRST CONTACTS

For many centuries the Chinese kept their technology within their own country. They considered their way of life so superior to that of other nations that they had no desire to travel or trade with foreign lands. Finally, in the second century B.C., a Chinese traveler named Chang Chhien set out on a long westward journey. He went as far as the present country of Afghanistan in Central Asia. From there he sent out exploring parties that reached the Persian

A scene along the Mian River
in modern China.

Gulf in the south and parts of what are now Iran and the Soviet Union to the north. His trip spread knowledge about China's marvelous civilization to the West; and Chang Chhien brought home information about civilizations beyond his country's borders.

Westerners were eager to obtain fine silk, pottery, and other products of Chinese technology, so traders began to make long journeys across the mountains and deserts of Central Asia. In Rome, the rich capital of the West, the fine silks from China were especially prized. At one point so much Roman gold was being exported to pay for them that the Emperor Tiberius, who ruled the Roman Empire at the time when Christ was crucified in Jerusalem, prohibited the wearing of silk in Rome in order to keep his gold supply from being depleted.

The mountains around the edges of China were high, and the trip across the burning deserts to the west of the country was long and hard. So contact between East and West remained infrequent until late in the thirteenth century. It was then that Marco Polo and his family made their famous journey to the Orient.

Although China went its own way for many more centuries after that, knowledge of its wonderful way of life and of the unbelievable inventions that the Chinese had been developing since ancient times spread rapidly to the West. There that knowledge had a profound effect on the future of the globe.

2

WONDERS OF CHINESE SCIENCE

Three Chinese inventions had far-reaching effects on people everywhere. These were gunpowder, the compass, and printing. The great English philosopher and historian Sir Francis Bacon (1561–1626) considered these developments so important that he called them the three inventions that changed the entire world.

GUNPOWDER

The first reference to gunpowder found anywhere in the world appears in a manual for Chinese **alchemists**, forerunners of modern chemists. (The word *chemistry* is derived from *alchemy*.) For centuries alchemists worked in crude laboratories, mixing together chemicals in an attempt to discover nature's deeper secrets. Many thought they could find a magical substance that would create gold from ordinary metals. Others searched for an exotic potion to prolong people's lives.

The first reference that the alchemists made to gunpowder was a warning for others *not* to make it! This warning, published in a ninth-century book, says that a mixture of charcoal, saltpeter, and sulfur might blow up in the alchemist's face. Such an accident, the manual warns, could "singe his beard" or even burn down an alchemist's laboratory.

Charcoal, saltpeter, and sulfur are the basic ingredients of gunpowder. Soon after its discovery, the Chinese began to use it on the battlefield. Early in the tenth century, Chinese armies carried fire lances to frighten off enemies. Fire lances were weapons made by packing gunpowder into a foot-long tube and placing it on the end of a lance. The soldiers lit the powder just before they charged.

Within a century the Chinese were packing gunpowder into bombs that they could throw at enemy troops, much as hand grenades are used in modern warfare. Chinese armies had long used toxic smoke screens against opponents. They created these screens by building fires and adding poisonous chemicals, such as arsenic, to them. In the twelfth century they added arsenic to gunpowder when building their grenadelike bombs. This marked the beginning of chemical warfare.

ROCKETS

The Chinese also used gunpowder in rockets, which they shot off to celebrate special occasions. It was only a short step to the use of these devices in warfare. By the late fourteenth century they had developed two-stage rockets. The first stage carried the "warhead" up over the advancing force; then the second stage released a hail of arrows that rained down on the enemy.

The Chinese built the first cannon in the thirteenth century; they used hollow bamboo tubes to shoot rocks and pieces of iron at their enemies. Metal cannon barrels first appeared in the East later in that century; this development traveled west to Europe within a few decades. In less than a hundred years such weapons were being used against castles, which had been hard to conquer earlier.

Above: *a three-shot
gun.* Right: *rockets
attached to arrows,
probably equipped
with poisoned tips*

In 1449 the king of France used cannon to knock down English castles in Normandy at the rate of five a month.

THE COMPASS

Another Chinese discovery that the nations of the West seized upon eagerly was the magnetic compass. Although magnetism had been known in both the East and West for several centuries before the birth of Christ, the Chinese were the first to use it.

As early as 300 B.C. the Chinese noticed that the iron ore called lodestone attracts pieces of metal. They also found that a piece of lodestone carved into the shape of a spoon always points in the same direction. A Chinese book written at the beginning of the Christian era mentions something called a "south-pointing spoon." This was the world's first compass.

Why a *south*-pointing spoon? You may think that a compass needle always points north, but it actually points both north and south at the same time. The Chinese chose to think of it pointing south instead of north.

Within a few centuries the Chinese had embedded pieces of lodestone into wooden blocks carved in the shape of a fish. These blocks were then placed in water. Sailors used south-pointing fish, as they called them, to find their way across the ocean on overcast days. Armies also used south-pointing fish to point the way over land during long marches in cloudy weather.

THE SOUTH-POINTING NEEDLE

Next, the Chinese discovered that they could magnetize a piece of metal by rubbing it against lodestone. They then replaced the south-pointing fish with a magnetized needle. In the eighth century A.D. all references in Chinese books to south-pointing fish were replaced by references to south-pointing needles.

*A working model of the
"south-pointing spoon,"
the oldest known compass*

The south-pointing needle, like a modern compass, always pointed toward the earth's magnetic poles (instead of "true" north and south). There is a difference of a few degrees between magnetic north and true north at most places on the globe. This difference, which is called **declination** today, changes as the observer moves to the east or west. The Chinese noticed this and wrote about it late in the eleventh century, some four hundred years before the West discovered compass declination during Columbus's historic voyage of discovery in 1492.

Although Marco Polo made no mention of the compass in his writings about China (he found his way across the trackless deserts of Central Asia by following the sun and stars), knowledge of the compass appeared in Europe at about the time he made his journey to the East. This knowledge was transmitted by the Arabs, who had been trading with the Chinese for centuries. In this way the magnetic compass arrived in Europe in time to help Columbus find the New World. It guided other sailors from Spain, Portugal, England, Holland, and France on their voyages of discovery to America and across the Indian Ocean to the East, where the compass had originated.

PRINTING

Over half a century before Columbus sailed westward, a German printer named Johannes Gutenberg (1400–1468) began working on another idea that eventually changed the world. This was printing with **movable type**. (It is called this because each letter is separate and is used over and over.) When he succeeded in printing a page with movable type during the 1430s, Gutenberg probably thought he had invented a new process. However, the Chinese had been using this kind of type for over four hundred years before Gutenberg began his experiments.

Printing has a long history in China, where people began writing things down 3,500 years ago. What we call India ink was actually developed in China long before the birth of Christ. Chinese scholars used brushes and ink to draw elaborate written characters on sheets of bamboo, on thin pieces of wood, or on silk. In this way they began creating books over two thousand years ago.

About A.D. 100 a government official named Ts'ai Lun created paper by combining mulberry pulp with old rags and hemp. By the second century A.D. the Chinese were using both ink and paper, two of the three things needed for the printing process.

Their next step was to reproduce the religious texts that had been carved on marble pillars in temples. Visiting pilgrims began rubbing ink over these raised surfaces and pressing paper against the inked characters to transfer the message to the paper. By the

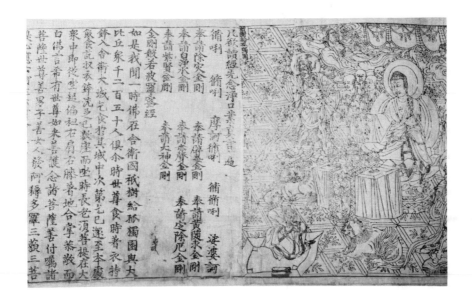

A page from the earliest dated printed book

fourth or fifth century A.D. a similar process was being used to print from seals carved in clay or wood.

In the sixth century the Chinese began printing entire pages from wood blocks. The text was first written in ink on a sheet of paper. This sheet was pressed against a wood block coated with rice paste to retain the ink. Then the wood around the characters was carved away, leaving the raised text with the characters reversed. The printer would coat the raised surface with ink and press a sheet of paper against it. This printed the entire page at one time.

The secret of printing soon became known throughout the East. The oldest known printed work comes from China's neighbor, Japan. There a Buddhist chant was printed between A.D. 764 and 770. The oldest known Chinese book, a religious text, was printed in A.D. 868. Less than a century later, in A.D. 932, the Chinese used the wood block method to print a collection of their classics that ran to over a hundred volumes.

MOVABLE TYPE

Movable type was the next logical development. Between 1041 and 1048 a Chinese alchemist named Pi Shêng conceived the idea of using movable type in printing. Pi Shêng made his characters out of clay hardened by baking.

Printing with movable type was not as useful in China as it was in Europe because Chinese writing contains 80,000 different symbols instead of the twenty-six letters of the Roman alphabet. So wood blocks continued to be important in Chinese printing for some time along with movable type.

In 1313 a Chinese magistrate named Wang Chen had a craftsman carve more than 60,000 wooden characters for him to use in printing a history of technology. In 1403 the king of Korea ordered a set of 100,000 pieces of type cast in bronze. Other sets of metal type were created in the East early in the fifteenth century.

Printing was so important to the Chinese that until the end of the eighteenth century there were more books in China alone than could be found in all the other countries of the world combined. As printing spread throughout the West after Gutenberg's invention (or reinvention) of movable type, more and more books were printed there. These books played an important part in the rapid expansion of learning that accompanied the rebirth of Western civilization that is today called the Renaissance.

3

SCANNING
THE HEAVENS

Technological progress was important to the Chinese, but from ancient times they also applied themselves to pure science. Astronomy, the study of the stars, was one pure-science field.

Marco Polo described thirteenth-century Beijing as a city of about five thousand stargazers, all interested in the movements of heavenly bodies for one reason or another. Some of them were astrologers, who fancied they could discover what to expect in the future by plotting the movements of the stars and planets. Others were astronomers, who carefully measured the orbits of distant celestial bodies and predicted tides, seasonal changes, and other natural events on earth by the things they learned from their study of the stars. These thirteenth-century astronomers came from a long line of scientists that stretches back to prehistoric times. Some of the earliest accurate stellar observations recorded anywhere in the world were made by these ancient stargazers.

PRACTICAL NEEDS

The accurate observation of heavenly bodies is necessary for many reasons. Farmers need a calendar to tell them when it is safe to plant their crops in the spring without danger of frost or freezing weather. Spring floods are caused by melting snow in far-off mountains. Floods can be predicted with reasonable accuracy if people keep track of the months that pass to know when such events generally occur. China has always depended on its farmers to produce food for the many people who live there, so an astronomer who could devise an accurate calendar received high honors in ancient times.

Other, more subtle knowledge can be gained by observing the skies. A priest or king who can predict eclipses of the sun or moon will seem to possess divine knowledge. Those who can forecast these events are often credited with being able to foretell other happenings. The common people often worship such leaders and are more likely to listen to their warnings and to obey their commands.

Tradition says that the first astronomical observatories in China were built over four thousand years ago by Huang-Ti, an emperor who, according to legend, also taught the people how to write, play music, and raise silkworms. There is no way to know if this is true; but the first Chinese writing, which was scratched onto bones over 3,500 years ago, shows that people already knew that the year is 365¼ days long. This is amazingly close to the length of the year as it is measured today (365.24219 days). It is also more accurate than calculations made by other people who lived that far back in time.

By the thirteenth century B.C. the Chinese had recorded the length of the lunar month as 29.53 days—extremely close to the 29.530879 days measured by modern scientists. (A lunar month is one revolution of the moon around the earth.) Chinese astronomers developed an accurate calendar with twelve lunar months in each year that started on the winter solstice. The winter solstice is the time around December 22 when the sun is at its southernmost point in the winter skies. Twelve lunar months gave them a year of

This writing has been scratched onto a piece of bone. It is 3,500 years old.

approximately 360 days. In order to adjust this to the true year, the emperor added an extra month from time to time (approximately once every seven years). He had to rely upon his astronomers to tell him when to insert this month, and that added to their prestige in royal circles.

STRANGE STELLAR EVENTS

Chinese astronomers began recording eclipses of the moon as far back as 1361 B.C. They noted an eclipse of the sun a century and a half later in 1217 B.C. and began keeping regular records of eclipses after that. As early as 1000 B.C. the Chinese could accurately predict when an eclipse of the sun or moon would occur from such observations. It would be another five hundred years before astronomers in the West learned how to do this.

Chinese astronomers also noticed that strange stars sometimes appear suddenly, burn brightly for a short time, then disappear. Called **guest stars**, the first of these to be recorded appeared in the vicinity of a star now called Antares around 1300 B.C. The newcomer lasted for only two days.

Today we would call a guest star a nova. Dozens of times every year, distant stars exhaust the nuclear fuel that makes them burn. Just before collapsing, such stars explode. They appear to burn more brightly (to the naked eye) for a brief time before disappearing from view.

Once every century or two a much more powerful explosion called a supernova is seen. The first supernova explosion ever recorded occurred in June 1054 A.D., when a star in the constellation Taurus suddenly flared up. Chinese observers reported that it was as bright as Venus, that it could be seen during daylight hours, and that it sent out reddish-white flares that were visible for twenty-three days. The remnant of this explosion can be seen today and is called the Crab Nebula.

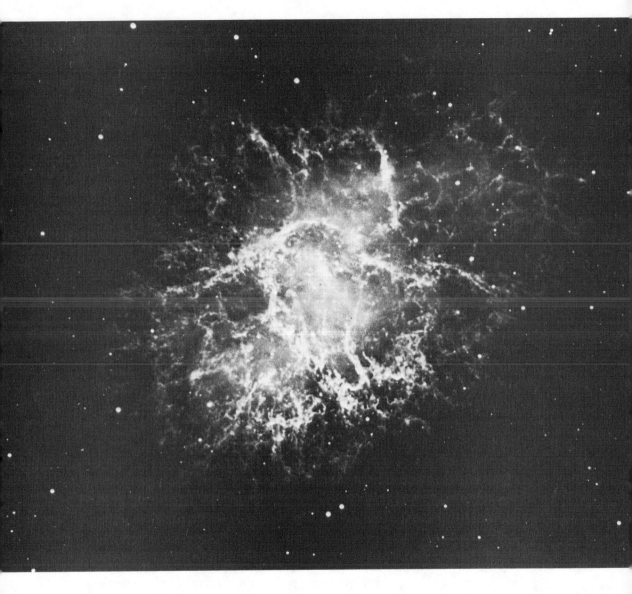

The Crab Nebula, whose appearance in A.D. 1054
was recorded by Chinese astronomers

The Chinese also observed and recorded sunspots, which are caused by flares on the surface of the sun. They saw comets, which pass near the solar system from distant space. Halley's Comet, which last swung around the sun in the winter of 1985–86, has returned to the solar system at intervals of approximately seventy-five years throughout the ages. The Chinese observed a comet that may have been Halley's in the year 467 B.C. Another sighting in 240 B.C. was definitely this comet; the Chinese kept records of many visits by Halley's and other comets during the centuries that followed. By the sixth century A.D. they had realized that these celestial wanderers reflect the sun's light rather than shining on their own. A thousand years earlier, in the fourth century B.C., they had figured out that the moon reflects the light of the sun instead of producing its own energy.

OBSERVATORIES
AND INSTRUMENTS

Over a thousand years before the birth of Christ the stargazers of ancient China began studying the stars from observatories throughout the land. These observatories allowed them to accurately plot the movements of the moon, planets, and visiting comets against the background of the stars that have relatively fixed positions. By the fifth century B.C. Chinese astronomers had catalogued 1,464 stars and divided them into constellations that they named and wrote about.

The observatories could be established because China was already a well-organized nation. Organization allowed the Chinese to send out scientific expeditions long before other nations. In the eighth century A.D. the great Chinese astronomer and mathematician I-Hsing led a group that surveyed the arc of a meridian of longitude that stretched south from Mongolia to the area where Vietnam is now located, a distance of around 1,500 miles (2,500

Thirteenth-century astronomical instruments
used to plot the movements of the earth,
planets, sun, and stars

km). Meridians of longitude are imaginary lines running north and south between the poles of the earth. Navigators use them to determine where they are, and astronomers can estimate the size of the earth by measuring the distance along these lines.

At about the same time another Chinese expedition traveled to an area near present-day Singapore to study constellations in the Southern Hemisphere. Such stars cannot be seen in the Northern Hemisphere because they are below the horizon there.

To study the stars the Chinese developed several instruments. The simplest and most ancient was a vertical pole, called a **gnomon**. With a gnomon they could check the sun's shadow and keep track as it lengthened toward its longest point at the winter solstice. They could also watch it get shorter and shorter as the summer solstice in June approached. This simple instrument allowed them to measure the length of the year with accuracy over three thousand years ago. Inscriptions from the thirteenth century B.C. show a diagram of a person holding such a pole, which gives an indication of the age of this instrument.

To be accurate a gnomon had to be exactly vertical. The Chinese assured verticality by dangling a weight on a cord; this gave them a line that was straight up and down. The surface where the shadow was cast had to be exactly horizontal; the Chinese accomplished this by means of a trough of water that would reveal any slant or other irregularity.

About 500 B.C. a Chinese astronomer named Tsu Kêng Chih made a vertical gnomon and horizontal measuring scale out of bronze. He combined these into one instrument, which made possible measurements even more accruate than the older systems. Another way to increase the accuracy of the measurements was to

A gnomon

The Tower of Chou Kung, used for measuring the lengths of sun shadows, was built in A.D. 1276 in a place once thought to be the center of the world. A gnomon stood in the space running down the front of the tower. The tower is 40 feet (12 m) high.

use bigger and bigger gnomons. The Chinese constructed huge buildings 40 to 50 feet (10 to 15 m) high with areas beside them where a shadow could be carefully measured and calibrated.

Sighting tubes were used by the ancient Chinese when observing the stars. Although these tubes did not contain lenses like those in modern telescopes, they helped them see faint stars by shutting out light from surrounding celestial bodies and earthly objects. The tubes also allowed for accurate tracking of stars and made possible better measurement of their angles above the nightly horizon. The Chinese knew they should not look directly at the sun to observe an eclipse or sunspots, so they viewed these phenomena through translucent rock crystals or transparent jade.

COSMIC VIEWS

As the Chinese accumulated more and more knowledge about the heavenly bodies, some of their philosophers formulated ideas about the nature of the universe. Throughout their long history the Chinese people have basically had three different theories about the cosmos.

The oldest of these was that the earth, which they thought of as being flat or slightly curved, floated on water. Overhead, the sky was a curved dome; the stars were fixed to its surface. The sun and moon had movements of their own, crossing this domed sky at regular intervals.

By the second century B.C. the Chinese had altered their view of the universe. They began to think of it as a giant egg. The earth was the yolk at the center of this curved universe. Around the earth stretched the curved sky like the inside of an eggshell. The Chinese calculated the size of this universe, giving the diameter of the egg as 2,032,300 **li**, or approximately 700,000 miles (over 1 million km). (A li is a unit of Chinese measurement equal to approximately one-third of a mile, or about 500 km.) Philosophically, the Chinese admitted that they had no idea what lay beyond the celestial "egg."

In the third century A.D. the Chinese came up with their third and final version of what the cosmos is like. Called the Hsüan Yeh, or "infinite, empty space" teaching, this theory held that the blue sky that seems to arch overhead is an optical illusion. Instead, they said, space goes on and on. By the eighth century they added that this universe had existed for a hundred million years.

These theories gave the Chinese a framework to go along with their observations of the phenomena that they saw in the skies. However, most of China's astronomers concentrated on cataloging celestial events and figuring out calendars for the farmers to use on earth, preferring to leave philosophical questions about the universe to those who wanted to investigate such matters.

4

BASIC SCIENCE AND MATHEMATICS

While some of China's ancient scientists searched the skies to learn the secrets of the stars and planets, others probed about on earth to find answers to the riddles of nature. These researchers knew nothing about many basic scientific concepts that every schoolchild learns today.

FIVE ELEMENTS

The Chinese had no idea that matter is made up of tiny atoms held together by fields of force. Nor did they know that these atoms form over a hundred elements that are the basic building blocks of all material things.

Instead, China's learned people of three thousand years ago thought that all things were made up of five elements: fire, earth, metal, water, and wood. They looked at the changes that took place in these five things and tried to explain nature in terms of these changes. Wood undergoes a basic change to produce fire (flames); fire changes to earth (ashes); earth produces metal (iron and other ores are mined from the ground); metal produces water (dew collects on metal surfaces exposed overnight); and completing the circle, water produces wood (woody plants need water to grow).

The Chinese scientists who lived many centuries ago looked at the five elements *not* as static building blocks of the universe but as changing objects in a changing world. Heated objects cool; cold things can be heated. Rain falls on dry earth and wets it; the sun shines on wet ground and dries it. Chinese scientists saw that seeds placed in the earth grow into plants that then die and replenish the soil so that more plants can grow. Everywhere around them the ancient Chinese saw changes going on in nature.

These changes were a fundamental part of ancient Chinese thought, which saw them as involving an interplay of two basic forces called **yin** and **yang**. This concept is still important in Chinese thought. Yin involves cold, wet, passive things and forces; in people it represents femininity and intuitive ways of thinking. Yang pertains to warm, dry, active things in nature, to masculinity, and to the intellectual side of all individuals. The sun, which produces light and heat, is yang; the moon, which reflects light, is yin. Yang pertains to day; yin to night.

All things contain both yin and yang. One or the other of these will predominate most of the time, making a person or object more yang or yin. Yin and yang are not two separate things but different manifestations of the same basic force in nature.

Yin and yang working together produce the **Tao** (pronounced *dow*). Tao, generally translated as "the way" or "the path," is the course that all things follow when they are in tune with nature. One of the objects of ancient Chinese science was to discover the Tao of a thing or an idea or, better yet, to find the Tao of nature as a whole.

THE *BOOK OF CHANGES*

One of the earliest attempts of the Chinese to build an orderly system of knowledge around this interplay of yin and yang was a book called the *I Ching,* or *Book of Changes.* The origin of the *I Ching* (pronounced *ye ching*), like the origins of yin and yang, of the Tao, and of the five elements, is lost in antiquity. Legends say that the book was written by a ruler named King Wen some three or four thousand years ago. Modern scholars think the *I Ching* was actually written down (perhaps from older oral sources) sometime between the sixth and eighth centuries B.C.

The *I Ching* consists of sixty-four hexagrams. These are characters with six lines that look like this:

$$\overline{}\;\overline{}\;\overline{}\;\overline{}\;\overline{}\;\overline{}$$

or this:

or this:

The solid lines are yang lines; the broken ones are yin. The *I Ching* combines yin and yang into an organized system. These hexagrams are thought of as an organized way to look at all natural phenomena in the world and to get in tune with the collected wisdom of the ages. Science has always attempted to do this, using different systems and techniques throughout history.

Many of the ancient concepts were organized into an orderly way of looking at the universe by the fourth-century B.C. scholar Tsou Yen, who is often considered the founder of Chinese scientific thought. Tsou Yen, whose exact birth and death dates are unknown, wrote about the theory of the five elements. He laid down a system of rules for classifying most large and small objects. His writing includes essays on the interplay of yin and yang; in them he discussed how these forces could best be applied to scientific work.

ALCHEMY

Among Tsou Yen's many writings are some of the first on alchemy to be found anywhere in the world. Alchemists, in addition to searching for ways to create gold from base metals and for a magical *elixir* to extend life, also tried to find explanations for the phenomena that they saw in the natural world around them.

Tsou Yen listed many of the natural products, such as minerals and herbs, that the alchemists of his time worked with in their search.

Although some alchemists wanted to cheat rulers and other rich people with false claims that they could make gold, others honestly believed in what they were doing. To change one metal into another seemed possible within the framework of knowledge that people had at the time.

For example, the Chinese found out over three thousand years ago that copper and tin—two relatively soft metals—could be

An alchemist refining silver

combined to form bronze, a metal hard enough to be made into swords, shields, spears, and ordinary digging tools. Just as copper and tin seemed to lose their basic property of softness and become a third and harder substance, alchemists believed the same thing could happen when other substances were combined. Potters converted ordinary clay into beautiful vases by glazing and firing them; and iron was hardened into steel by heating it in charcoal. So, why shouldn't it be possible to change base metals into gold?

Early in their experiments the ancient Chinese alchemists found that they could create a metal that resembled gold by combining copper with either zinc carbonate or other substances containing zinc. This mixture is called brass today. Other combinations yielded metals that looked like silver. A mixture of about 2 percent arsenic and 98 percent copper produces a beautiful, golden-colored metal. However, if the percentage of arsenic in the **alloy** is increased to over 4.5 percent, the result is a metal with a shiny, silverlike effect.

DEADLY ELIXIRS

From the idea of creating gold, the most perfect of metals, alchemists evolved the idea that they could bring about basic changes within people's bodies. Such changes, they thought, would extend life and might perhaps produce eternal life right here on earth. They believed that old people could be rejuvenated and their own physical and mental powers increased. This led to a search for an **elixir of life**, a substance that could cure all of people's ills, extend life, restore youth, and perhaps even do all three of these things.

Many elixirs worked for a while because they contained alcohol, arsenic, or other drugs that gave the user a temporary lift. The alchemists experimented with arsenic over and over. It worked well in making cheaper metals look like gold, so the alchemists reasoned that it could also do wonderful things for people who drank it. Arsenic is poisonous, but when drunk in small quantities it produces a temporary feeling of well-being. Many alchemists thought that if a little arsenic did this, more would bring about the effect they wanted. There is no way of knowing how many people the alchemists killed in their efforts to create an elixir of life.

Some of the alchemists were women. One was Kêng Hsien-Seng, who lived about the middle of the ninth century A.D. She became so well known that the emperor summoned her to court, where she told fortunes and performed various acts of what appeared to be magic. Kêng Hsien-Seng also prepared elixirs of life and experimented with changing cheap metals into gold. Another female alchemist was Li Shao-Yum, who lived in the twelfth century. She dressed in Taoist robes and wandered from temple to temple in a region of south-central China mixing elixirs, writing poems, and probably telling fortunes, as was the custom of the day.

Out of the work of the alchemists came a knowledge of how to combine metals and other substances to produce alloys for ordinary use. Their work also helped the Chinese produce the colorful dyes, varnishes, and glazes that made their vases and other products famous throughout the world. The study of herbs and drugs was useful in medicine. However, for the most part, alchemy as it was practiced in China—and later in the West—turned out to be a blind alley that science traveled until it changed into the modern experimental techniques of chemistry much later on.

ANCIENT NUMBERS

A system of numbers was essential to ancient China's search for nature's secrets because so much of science depends upon mathematical notations and calculations. Astronomers needed mathematics to compute the length of months and years, and early alche-

A page from a fourteenth-century book on algebra.
You can see the zeroes in the boxes. You can easily
pick out the numbers 1 and 2: | and | |. Negative
numbers have a slash through them: ++++ is −4.

mists depended upon fractions and other numerical notations for recording their secret formulas. So China's ancient scientists developed mathematical systems to describe what they did, as evidenced by early records showing the results of their calculations. An examination of these early records shows that over three thousand years ago the Chinese people used the same basic way of counting and figuring that they use today.

This system consists of nine basic numbers like that found throughout the modern world. By moving these numbers to the left or right, the same basic figures can symbolize units, tens, hundreds, thousands, and so on. The ancient Chinese scholar wrote 547 by putting down seven units, four tens, and five hundreds just as anyone does today. Numbers running into the millions and billions could be worked with. For many years the Chinese used a space where Western mathematicians used a circle. They adopted the round symbol for the zero in the eighth century A.D.

The Chinese used arithmetic to figure out everyday problems, such as how much dirt they would have to move to make a canal or to build a wall. They learned to figure out the area of a field by measuring two of its sides and the volume of dirt in a pile by measuring its sides and its height. They also computed taxes owed to the government, amounts of grain in the emperor's storehouse, and percentages and proportions owed a landlord by a tenant. By the first century A.D. they had computed the ratio between the diameter and circumference of a circle, the number that we call pi today; they carried it out to three decimal places. By the third century a Chinese mathematician named Liu Hui computed the value of pi as 3.14159, close to the figure used today.

Fractions were generally avoided by people in ancient times. Instead, they developed smaller and smaller units of measure to avoid having to deal with quantities that were less than a single unit. The Chinese were an exception; they had no problem with fractions. Around 1000 B.C. they divided the year into 365¼ days, and they continued to use fractions in their sales of grain and when distributing the profits of such transactions among a group of people.

Trigonometry—the branch of mathematics that deals with triangles and the relationships between their sides and angles—was very important to the mathematicians of ancient China. They were familiar with right triangles from their use of gnomons in astronomy. Chinese surveyors also used triangles to measure heights and to find distances across rivers or swampy areas when no one could pace them off. Their method for doing this was basically the same as that used today by Boy Scouts and Girl Scouts to measure the heights of trees or buildings.

To find the height of a tree one first measures a line running out from the tree and drives a peg into the ground. Next, he or she sights the angle between the ground at this peg and the top of the tree being measured. Since the tree and the ground form a right angle, the person now knows two of the three angles and the distance across the bottom of the triangle created by the tree, the ground, and a slanting line down from its top to the peg. With this information the height of the tree can be computed, either by using a mathematical formula or by drawing a triangle to scale on a piece of paper and actually measuring it.

To find the distance across a river, one selects an object on the other side, such as a rock or a tree. He or she faces it, then turns at a right angle (90 degrees) and measures off a line along the river. (This line can be any reasonable length.) Then the angle from the end of that line to the rock or tree on the other side is measured. Again, once a side and two angles are known, it is easy to compute the lengths of the other sides of the triangle, including the one that represents the distance from the starting point to the rock or tree on the other side.

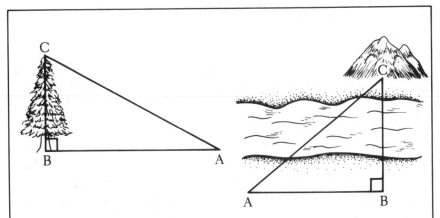

The Chinese used triangulation to measure everything from the height of a tree to the width of a river. Once angle B is fixed at 90 degrees and angle A and the distance from A to B are measured, the distance from B to C can be calculated.

A Chinese book called *Nine Chapters on the Mathematical Arts* gave rules for finding distances this way, as well as the area of rectangles, triangles, and circles. The book also told how to use fractions, work out percentages, use square and cube roots, and figure the volume of cones, pyramids, and cubes. It supplied useful mathematical information needed to distribute grain, build walls, and remove earth for canals. Liu Hui wrote an introduction to the work in the third century A.D. in which he said that the book had been written about five hundred years earlier.

In the second century B.C. the Chinese tried to use the triangular method to measure the distance from the earth to the sun, but their calculations were unsuccessful. This was partially due to the great distance involved and partly because they failed to allow for the curvature of the earth.

An abacus

When computing mathematical problems, the ancient Chinese used counting rods to add, subtract, multiply, and divide. These are short sticks that one lays out on the ground or on a table. One pile represents the units and is turned one way; another pile is the tens and is turned crosswise. The hundreds go into a third pile, the thousands into a fourth one, and so on. For example, 645 is laid out with five rods for the units, four for the tens, and six for the hundreds. Another figure can be added to it simply by laying down more rods for the hundreds, tens, and units in the appropriate piles. When ten or more units have been laid on the table, the mathematician takes up ten counting rods from that pile and adds one rod to the stack representing the tens. This is also done for the tens, hundreds, thousands, and so on. By the third century B.C. the Chinese had learned to add, subtract, multiply, divide, and do square roots with this system.

From counting rods it was easy to change over to an **abacus** in the fifth or sixth century A.D. An abacus has beads strung on wires that are used like counting rods. They are moved over to represent units, tens, hundreds, thousands, and so on. Each new number is added by moving beads, which is faster than working with the counting rods. The abacus is still used today.

5

HEALING THE PEOPLE

The beginnings of Chinese medicine, like so many things about ancient China, are hidden by the mists of time. Scholars know that doctors in China were using certain treatments over four thousand years ago because they have found physical evidence to support ancient legends describing the methods that were used.

The forces of yin and yang have been important in Chinese science and philosophy since ancient times; they were equally important in Chinese medicine. All illness was thought to result from an imbalance of yin and yang within a person's body. Chinese doctors worked to balance the twin forces within the person's body. Some of the ancient medical treatments described below are still in use.

ACUPUNCTURE AND MOXA

To restore the balance of yin and yang within a person's body, Chinese doctors used two main treatments: **acupuncture** and **moxa.** Acupuncture consists of sticking needles into a person at certain points on the body. Moxa (also called moxibustion) involves burning a fine tinder substance in an incenselike cone as it

An acupuncture figure.
The lines represent the
paths of the ch'i, or
life force, within the
body, and the points
on the lines represent
energy centers or
nerve endings.

is held just above one of the acupuncture points. The heat can be either great or slight, depending on how close the cone is brought to the body. Acupuncture was generally used for acute diseases, the kind that strike quickly and reach a crisis immediately. Moxa was applied in cases of chronic, or lingering, illnesses.

Both practices are very old. The Chinese attribute their discovery to Huang-Ti, the mythical emperor who is said to have built the first Chinese astronomical observatories over four thousand years ago. Archaeological evidence corroborates that the practices are indeed very old. The Chinese originally used bone needles for acupuncture; they changed over to metal ones when they learned to use bronze and copper about 3,500 years ago. The needles they used were and are so thin and sharp that they cause little or no pain when a doctor pushes them deep into places on the body that are thought to be points where yin and yang can be influenced. The Chinese believe that these needles affect the flow of a life force within the body that is related to the yin and yang of nature. They call this life force the ch'i.

THE CIRCULATORY SYSTEM

Their belief in the ch'i was and is central to Chinese medicine. The ch'i is said to ebb and flow as the yin and yang do in nature. There are actually two kinds of ch'i: the yin-ch'i and the yang-ch'i. Their interest in the movement of the ch'i within the body led Chinese doctors to an extremely important medical discovery: the circulation of the blood.

Medical books written in China during the first century B.C. described the two kinds of ch'i and their relationship to the blood. The yin-ch'i was said to circulate inside the blood vessels, while the yang-ch'i moved outside them. A couple of centuries later the Chinese said that the motion of the ch'i in the body depends upon the circulation of the blood, which flows continuously in one direction, stopping only when a person dies. These statements were written over fifteen hundred years before the English doctor William Harvey (1578–1657) "discovered" the circulation of the blood for European medicine.

Once the Chinese understood that blood circulates, they tried to measure it and to find out how fast it travels through the veins and arteries. They concluded that the blood circulates throughout the body about fifty times each day. It actually takes only thirty seconds to completely circulate. However, the ancient Chinese were right about its continuous flow in one direction. From there they learned much more about how the arteries and veins work.

Knowledge about the blood's circulation allowed the Chinese to develop surgical techniques at an early stage in their history. In the third century A.D. they also invented a wine that produced general anesthesia in patients. This enabled them to perform operations that were impossible in the West before the nineteenth century.

MEDICINAL HERBS

Along with acupuncture, moxa, and surgery, Chinese medicine made widespread use of herbs, plants believed to have healing qualities. Herbs were used in Chinese medicine before the dawn of written history. According to legend, a mythical emperor named Shen Nung (who lived around the time of Huang-Ti) first taught people how to select the correct plants to use. Later, alchemists experimented with herbs in their search for the magical elixir of life. They found some that could ease pain, others that reduced fever, and some that treated colds or filled other sickroom needs. This knowledge became a carefully guarded secret; it appeared in books only after it had become general knowledge throughout the country. Herbal knowledge was finally collected in a book during the sixth century A.D. by a doctor named T'ao Hung Ching. His book described 730 herbs and drugs used in Chinese medicine at that time.

Medical knowledge was passed along from one person to another in ancient China. However, the Chinese established a system to examine and license doctors several centuries before the Christian era. The actual training of physicians remained a matter of passing along information from one generation to another until the tenth century A.D., when the first medical school was started in China. By that time the nation's doctors also knew how to inoculate people against smallpox, a practice that the West knew nothing about for another nine hundred years.

The Chinese had only hazy ideas about how diseases spread from one person to another; they also had little knowledge about sanitation. Yet they discovered that homes in which sick people died should be fumigated by burning a chemical inside to create a poisonous smoke. Called the "fire treatment," this form of fumigation orginated several centuries before the Christian era.

The Chinese discovered other ways to prevent the spread of disease as well. In the year A.D. 980 a Chinese monk named Tsan-Ning wrote that during an epidemic people should collect the clothes of a sick person and steam them as soon as possible. He said that this would keep others in the family from catching the disease. These writings predate by almost nine hundred years the work of Joseph Lister (1827–1912), who pioneered the use of antiseptic practices in the operating rooms of Western hospitals.

6

FEEDING THE PEOPLE

Early in their history the Chinese used primitive forms of technology to produce food. Over time they progressed from simple techniques to increase crop production to fairly complex practices such as irrigation and flood control.

While most of the world's people were still gathering roots and berries in the woods or hunting, the Chinese began growing crops in the rich river valleys of Eastern Asia. Ancient legends say that **millet**, a grain, fell from the sky, and that the mythical emperor Shen Nung collected and cultivated it. Legends also credit him with inventing the wooden plow, the hoe, and other implements needed to cultivate fields.

EARLY BEGINNINGS

He is supposed to have done so over four thousand years ago, which indicates that the Chinese think these technologies are very old. Modern research by archaeologists confirms this; the practices of tilling the soil and producing grain in China go back at least a thousand years *before* that mythical time, according to them.

For example, archaeologists have found millet in Chinese burial sites that are much older than any written history. Even wheat, which originated in the Middle East, has been found in the burial sites of early Stone Age people who roamed parts of China. Thus, the origin of agriculture—the practice of producing food instead of merely searching for it in the fields and forests—is so ancient that we can only guess how it actually began.

Scientists do know that the practice of growing crops was invented independently in several places in the world. These include China, the Middle East, Egypt, and parts of North and South America. These scientists also speculate that some ancient person probably gathered seeds in the wild and brought them back to camp. Some of the seeds may have been spilled at the edge of the place where people lived. In time they would have sprouted and grown there. This probably happened many times before people got the idea of growing food right at the edge of camp instead of searching for it in the fields and forests. This information would then have been passed down from generation to generation, and decades of trial and error may have gone into finding out the best kinds of seeds to use and how to go about cultivating them for best results.

VALLEY CIVILIZATIONS

China's early farmers were concentrated in the Yellow River valley in the north and in the Yangtze River region farther south. At about the time when some of these farmers began to produce millet, wheat, and rice, others started domesticating dogs and pigs. Sometime after that, cows were also domesticated; then oxen were hitched to crude wooden plows used to till the soil. Early in China's agricultural history, farmers added soybeans to the grains they were growing. Soybeans, a good source of protein, were ground into meal, eaten as sprouts, or turned into a milky curd and eaten with rice or other grains.

The yearly floods in the river valleys leave behind deposits of rich soil washed down from the mountains of the west. Such river silt is rich in minerals such as potassium, phosphorus, and calcium, the soil nutrients needed to grow plants. By adding animal manure to this soil, the farmers of ancient China were able to produce bigger and better crops.

By the fourth century B.C. the Chinese had developed a productive system of agriculture. They gave careful attention to the correct dates for plowing the land and planting the kinds of seeds that gave them best results. In addition, farmers in many areas raised two or three crops each year, squeezing maximum production from their fields.

Also during the fourth century B.C. the Chinese began to replace wooden implements with plows made from cast iron. This allowed them to plow more deeply, a practice that further increased crop production.

FLOOD CONTROL

China's food supply was threatened by seasonal droughts when there was not enough water and by floods when there was too much. These extremes were made even worse by the great inequities in rainfall over the large and varied country. The drier areas around Beijing in the north get as little rainfall as 10 to 20 inches (25 to 50 cm) per year, while the extreme southeast around Guangzhou gets 60 to 80 inches (150 to 200 cm) of rain each season.

The Chinese used their knowledge of technology to cope with this situation by building dams and reservoirs along the Yellow River as early as 1000 B.C. These dams and reservoirs allowed

Terraced farming in modern China

people to store water for irrigation and also to control floods. Over the next few centuries the Chinese constructed an extensive system of dikes to keep the Yellow River within its banks during the rainy season. Farmers also began to terrace hillsides so that they could grow crops there. Terraces are nearly level areas that follow the curve of a hillside; the water running off a terraced field flows around the slope instead of going straight down it. This causes the water to run much more slowly, letting silt settle out along the way instead of being washed into the river below. More water also soaks into the ground, where crops can use it, instead of running off and being wasted.

The sighting tube, level, and vertical line, instruments used in astronomy, also made ideal surveying instruments. They were used to lay out terraces and to survey huge irrigation systems or flood-control projects. The Chinese also used their mathematical skills to figure out how much dirt would have to be moved when building dams and levees.

China's flood-control and irrigation systems were constantly threatened by seasonal downpours in the distant mountains where the long rivers begin. By maintaining rain gauges in the highlands

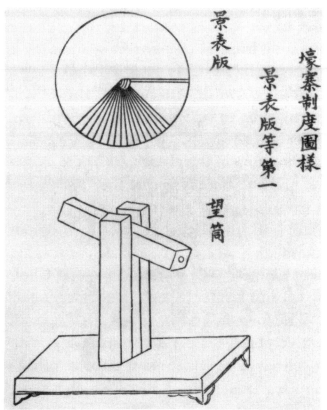

A sighting tube and a quadrant, an instrument used to measure angles

of Xizang to the west, government officials could judge when floods might occur and warn the people to reinforce their levees and take other precautionary measures.

OTHER TECHNOLOGIES

Much of China's rice was planted by hand because the work had to be done in flooded fields. Elsewhere, oxen were yoked together and used for plowing and cultivating the land. Horses were used less frequently, but when they were hitched to plows or used to pull loads, the Chinese used a harness that was much more effective than the kind of harness used in most cultures of the ancient world.

Most cultures used a harness that consisted of a throat strap around the animal's neck. This choked the horse when it pulled. During the fourth century B.C., while they were making many other agricultural advancements, the Chinese learned to use a harness that strapped around the horse's larger breast area instead of the throat. This greatly increased the efficiency of the harness, allowing the Chinese to use horses in their farming operations. A horse hitched with the Chinese breast-strap harness can pull 3,000 pounds (1350 kg) on level ground; one hitched with the more restrictive throat-strap harness can pull only half as much weight.

Also during the fourth century B.C. Chinese farmers began to lift water for irrigation with long sweeps. These devices had a bucket on one end and a counterweight on the other and made irrigation much easier. The pulley and windlass came into use a couple of centuries later as a way to draw up water from deep wells; at about the same time a hand crank was used to turn a rotary-fan winnowing machine that separated grain from chaff at harvest time.

The Chinese still use traditional iron plows.

Like farmers everywhere, the Chinese struggled to save their crops from insect pests. They developed a few poisons, such as arsenic, for this purpose. Natural insect controls were also used. A manuscript written in A.D. 340 tells of farmers in southern China buying little bags of ants at the central marketplace. These bags were hung in orange groves; there the ants kept down the mites and spiders that would have damaged the trees. This is the first known case in which insects were used to control other insects, a process known today as biological pest control.

FOOD AND POPULATION

As China's agricultural technology improved, allowing those who tilled the soil to produce more food, its population also increased. In 1000 B.C. China had about 6 million people. By the fourth century B.C. this figure had grown to 25 million. The increased use of irrigation that began in the fourth century B.C., together with the introduction at about the same time of iron plows, fertilizers, and other technologies, allowed more and more food to be grown. As a result, China's population doubled over the next several centuries. By A.D. 1, when China took its first official census, the country had 57 million people, a number that remained constant for the next thousand years.

7

DOWN-TO-EARTH DEVELOPMENTS

The technologies that allowed the Chinese to produce food so effectively also enabled them to build fine roads, canals, and walls. This was at a time when most countries had only narrow, winding trails.

China's wide, straight highways were marked with signposts and had milestones at regular intervals. Travelers found post offices and rest houses with eating, sleeping, and bathing accommodations less than one day's journey apart along the major routes.

Over these roads moved horse-drawn chariots and wagons pulled by oxen. Wealthy Chinese often sat in chairs or reclined in litters carried by porters when traveling. The poorer people walked along the side of the road, where they mingled with workers pushing carts and wheelbarrows.

ROAD-BUILDING TECHNIQUES

All roads had a prearranged width because the Chinese standardized the wheelspan of their chariots at approximately 5 feet (1.5 m), just as Western nations later standardized the wheelspan of railroad trains and track widths. Major roads were approximately 15 feet (4.5 m) wide so three chariots could pass abreast; minor roads were only one chariot wide.

From early times the Chinese paved their major highways. First, they dug out a roadbed and filled it with crushed rock. Over this they laid flat paving stones embedded in a mortar made by mixing together lime, sand, and gravel. As early as the third century B.C. China had over 4,000 miles (6,400 km) of paved roads. During the next five hundred years they expanded this network; it reached an estimated 25,000 miles (40,000 km) by the third century A.D.

China's roads connected walled cities that had clean, straight streets laid out in squares like modern ones. Bridges or ferries crossed rivers that blocked the way, providing continuous links in an orderly system of transportation.

Ancient China's postal system was one of the best that the world has ever known. Riders like those later used in the U.S. Pony Express system carried the mail on regular schedules. Posts along the way provided changes of horses; the riders were also relieved at regular intervals.

CHINA'S CANAL SYSTEM

The Chinese built a network of canals to carry heavy loads, such as the grain collected for taxes. One reason for building canals is that water transportation greatly increases the amount of goods that a horse can pull. For example, a pack horse can carry a load on its back up to approximately 250 pounds (110 kg). The same horse when hitched to a wagon can pull about five times as much on a dirt road and up to fifteen times as much, or a couple of tons, on a paved surface. When hitched to a barge on a canal or river, the same horse can pull a load of thirty to fifty tons, which is fifteen to twenty-five times as much as the horse could haul on land.

In the fifth century B.C. the Chinese constructed a canal to connect the Yellow River in the north with two other rivers. During the next eighteen centuries they extended this system into what became known as the Grand Canal. Approximately 1,100 miles (1,800 km) long when completed in the thirteenth century A.D., the Grand Canal covered a distance equivalent to that between New York to Florida. Locks, which the Chinese developed in the tenth century, lifted barges loaded with grain from sea level up 140 feet (42 m) to the canal's highest point.

Chinese engineers also built narrow roads across the mountainous sections of their country, connecting them with suspension bridges that hung from ropes across chasms. Such bridges carried foot traffic and pack animals. To build them, first someone used a bow and arrow to shoot a light line across the chasm. Then work crews pulled heavier ropes across. Finally, huge ropes that could support the bridge and all of its traffic were pulled into place. By the sixth century A.D. the Chinese had replaced the bigger ropes with iron chains that supported these bridges—a technique unknown in Europe for another thousand years.

WALLED CITIES

China's roads and canals connected cities ringed by walls for protection. Walls have been used since the earliest times in China. The ancient nomads who roamed the land long before the rise of a civilization over five thousand years ago built earthen barriers around their camps to protect themselves from enemies. From this practice came the habit of building walled cities, which first appeared in China around 1500 B.C.

These walls were constructed by first putting up wooden forms and tamping down earth in between them. Then the forms were removed, leaving a solid wall of earth. The wall was covered with either flat stones or adobe bricks baked from clay to keep enemies

NANKING

The Grand Canal

from cutting through the earthen core. City walls were often 50 feet (15 m) high and 65 feet (20 m) wide at the base, tapering to narrower widths at the top.

In the fourth century B.C. the Chinese built walls along their northern border. These kept out the nomadic foreign tribesmen who threatened the country from that area. Huge stone walls with earthen cores extended mile after mile along the ridges of the mountains, snaking their way up and down hillsides and out across the Gobi Desert in the West.

During the third century B.C. an emperor named Shih Huang Ti united all of China and joined together the walls that the others had built. The result was the Great Wall of China, one of the world's greatest engineering feats.

The main wall is 1,500 miles (2,400 km) long and 30 feet (9 m) high in most places, with 40-foot (12-m) towers along the way. It guards China's northern frontier, from Turkestan in the west to the Pacific Ocean in the east. The length of this main wall is equal to the highway distance across the United States from New York to the middle of Kansas.

HOUSES

In the earliest times that modern people know anything about, Chinese houses were built using the same process used to construct city walls: earth was packed down between two temporary forms. Later the Chinese developed another way to build houses. First they made a frame by setting up poles at each corner of the building. These poles were then connected by beams running between them at the top. This framework supported the roof of the house, and the walls were hung from it.

In this way the frame, and not the walls of the house, carried the weight of the roof. The outside of the house could be made of light wood in the warm southern areas. In the northern part of

China where the winters are quite cold, people used brick or packed earth to form walls to shield them from the cold winds. Interior walls were often only bamboo screens. These were rolled up during the day to form larger rooms and then put down at night for privacy.

The main piece of furniture inside the typical Chinese house was a bench called a **kang**. This served as both a bed and a table. It also heated the house, because the Chinese built a fire outside and piped in the hot air through openings under the kang.

This form of "central heating" was one of the few luxuries in the average Chinese home. However, the buildings themselves were well designed; the people constructed their homes with the same engineering skills that made possible the nation's huge network of roads and canals.

SILK

The Chinese also applied the practical technology used in building walls and roads to the manufacture of fine products. One of the best known of these is the lustrous cloth called silk. Long before most people in the West knew where China was located or what the people there looked like, the wealthy merchants of Greece, Rome, and Persia were crossing deserts and mountains to trade for this highly prized material.

No one knows when the Chinese first learned to raise silkworms, collect and unwind their cocoons, and weave a fine cloth from the tiny threads that silkworms produce. Tradition says that the legendary Emperor Huang-Ti taught them how to do this. Other legends say that it was Huang-Ti's wife, the Empress Hsi-lina Shih, who discovered the technique. Some versions of these myths cite the year 2640 B.C. as the time when this happened.

The exact truth about how the Chinese learned to raise silkworms and convert their cocoons into cloth may never be known, but we do know that silk production has flourished in the Yellow River valley area for over four thousand years.

Then as now the first step was to raise silkworms, which live on mulberry trees and feed on the leaves. The silkworm moth lays between two hundred and five hundred eggs, each about as big as a pinhead. The eggs hatch into larvae—wiggly creatures that look much like caterpillars.

A silkworm larva grows from about a quarter of an inch (6 mm) to three inches (80 mm) long in about six weeks. During that time it feeds on huge quantities of mulberry leaves. A growing silkworm caterpillar often eats *its own weight* in leaves each day.

After about six weeks of feeding and growing, the silkworm settles down on a leaf and begins to spin a cocoon around itself. The tiny silken thread that the insect wraps around and around its body makes a continuous strand from 1,200 to 3,000 feet (365 to 900 m) long. These cocoons are collected and heated to kill the larvae inside.

Then comes the tedious process of unwinding the tiny filament of silk without breaking it. The cocoons are soaked in hot water to loosen the sticky material that holds them together. Then the thread is unwound. A Chinese worker takes several cocoons at one time and twists their thin strands together to form the silken thread that will later be woven into cloth. The length of the thread depends on the number of cocoons; this will vary according to the use that is planned for the finished material.

In ancient China much of the silk was woven into cloth by people working in their own homes. Women usually unwound the cocoons by hand, but men often helped weave the threads into cloth. Looms used for the weaving process go back beyond recorded history although they were constantly being improved. Other labor-saving methods were gradually adopted to replace the slower hand methods of ancient times. A treatise written in A.D. 1090 describes a silk-winding device operated by a foot treadle.

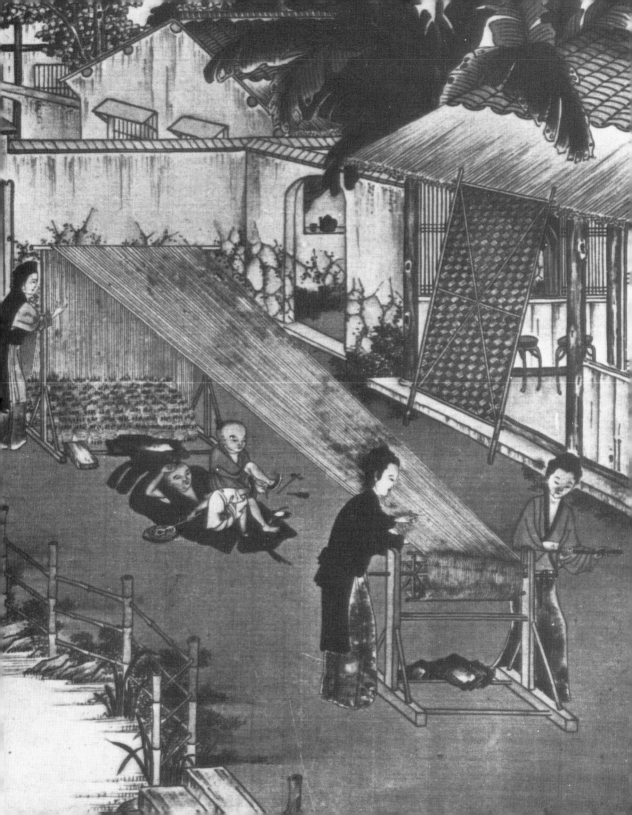

Spinning wheels, which are used to twist together short threads at the end of each cocoon, originated in India. They replaced hand-spinning techniques in China early in the thirteenth century. Water wheels came into use during the tenth and eleventh centuries to drive the silk-winding, spinning, and weaving machines.

PORCELAIN AND BRONZE

Another Chinese specialty is a fine pottery called porcelain. The Germans and Austrians later learned to produce fine porcelain pieces, but experts say that they have never been able to do as well as the Chinese did at the height of their porcelain production in the tenth century A.D. To this day fine dishes are still called china, regardless of whether they are made in the East or the West.

Pottery production in the East goes back beyond any historic record. Archaeological evidence shows that the people who lived along the Yellow River were making pots from clay at least four thousand years ago.

They used two kinds of clay. One was gray; Chinese artisans learned to coat it with glazes containing metallic elements that turned bright red or green or other pleasing colors when the piece was fired. A second kind of clay was white; from it they developed a delicate pottery so thin that light can shine through it. This could also be glazed to produce colorful vases and urns. From this clay

Silk thread is transferred from spools to a roll so that it can be woven into material.

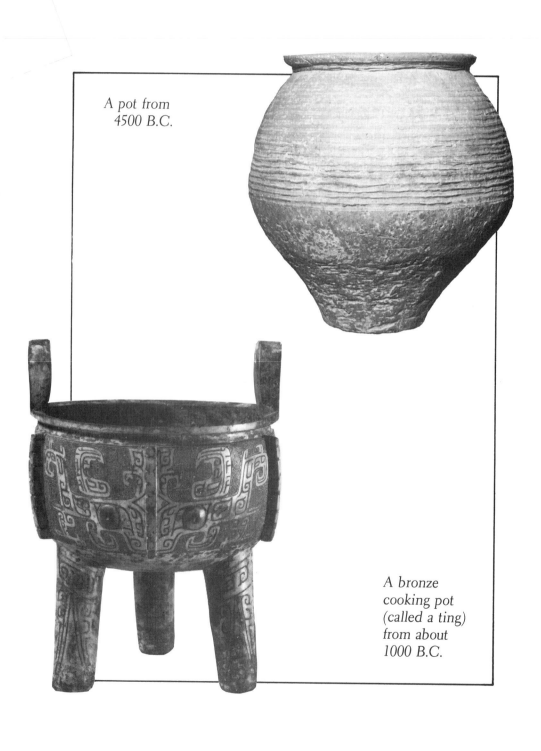

A pot from
4500 B.C.

A bronze
cooking pot
(called a ting)
from about
1000 B.C.

the Chinese produced the porcelain pieces that have been highly prized throughout history. Designs were painted on by workers using delicate brushes. So detailed and specialized was this work that an artist was trained for his or her entire lifetime in a particular type of design instead of trying to do a mixture of trees and animals or landscapes and plants.

Over three thousand years ago the Chinese created another specialty: casting fine bronze vases and figures. Bronze is the mixture of 80 to 85 percent copper and 15 to 20 percent tin that ancient peoples of many cultures learned to work long before they found out how to cast iron. Since it is softer, bronze is also more delicate than iron.

In order to make a fine bronze piece, an artisan first carved an exact model of the vessel in wax. All designs were carefully carved out or impressed on its surface. When the form was exactly right, the artisan began to brush on a mixture of clay and water so thin that it went into the tiniest openings. This was allowed to dry, and additional layers were brushed on.

Finally the clay was built up to a sufficient thickness. A few holes were left in the outside, and the clay was baked. The heat hardened the clay and melted the wax, which was drained out. Molten bronze, heated so that it flowed like a liquid, was then poured in the clay mold through the holes. When it cooled, the artisan had an exact copy in bronze of the original wax form.

The clay mold was broken away to reveal the bronze statue or urn beneath, so only one piece could be made from each mold. Holes left to drain out the wax and pour in the bronze were carefully filed and smoothed over. Then the finished piece was ready for the marketplace.

8

TOOLS AND TECHNOLOGY

The Chinese used engineering techniques found in few other ancient countries to produce fine products and to design their walls, roads, and canals. Some of these, like the hand tools they also devised, were unique to their way of life.

WHEELBARROWS AND WATER WHEELS

The wheelbarrow is such an invention; it appeared in China a thousand years before it was known in Europe. Tradition says that this implement, which the Chinese called the "wooden ox," was invented by an official named Chuko Liang in the third century A.D. However, it may have been known even earlier; carvings on Chinese tombs that show wheelbarrows being used go back at least two centuries before Chuko Liang's time.

Unlike the wheelbarrows used today in the West, which have a wheel in the front, the Chinese wooden ox had its wheel in the middle. The load was balanced in front and behind this wheel. The wheel supported the entire load, and the operator thus only had to steady the wheelbarrow and guide it. Wheelbarrows were also used to carry people; the Chinese added other interesting developments as well. They hitched horses to some wheelbarrows to pull loads, and by the thirteenth century a few ingenious people were also using sails!

Other inventions included the water wheel, which appeared in both the East and the West at about the beginning of the Christian era. Westerners used it to grind grain, but the Chinese began using water power to run bellows on furnaces where they heated cast iron.

Iron had been introduced into China in the sixth century B.C., about six hundred years after it was first used by a people called the Hittites in the Middle East. The Chinese used cast iron for tools and statues, fanning the fire where they heated it with a bellows powered at first by hand and later with water power.

FROM STEEL
TO SEISMOGRAPHS

In the second century B.C. the Chinese began heating iron in charcoal. This gave their metal the proper carbon content to make steel, which is harder than cast iron. Steel bits could be used to drill wells as deep as 2,000 feet (600 m). Many of these wells were used to supply water for entire villages; others brought up brine that was processed into salt.

To drill the deep wells, a group of people would jump on and off each end of a crossbeam to give it the up-and-down motion needed for drilling. Meanwhile, others rotated the drill cable so that the bit would cut into the earth. This is essentially the same process used almost two thousand years later in the southwestern United States to drill some of that country's first oil wells. In the United States it was called "kicking down" a well.

Chinese ingenuity also developed many things that people would later take for granted, such as accurate clocks. Like the ancient Egyptians, the Chinese had known about water clocks for

centuries. These devices work by letting water drip out of a container at a constant rate. Numbers marked on the side of the container indicate the time. Water clocks are not very accurate, but they were useful during nighttime hours when people cannot see the sun.

In the eighth century A.D. the Chinese astronomer and mathematician I-Hsing, who measured the arc of a meridian from Mongolia to Vietnam, took the water clock one step further. Working with a companion named Liang Ling-Tsan, he added an intricate set of gears to a water wheel that turned at a constant speed. These gears slowed down the motion from the water wheel so it could turn the hand of a clock at a pace that moved the marker around the dial only once a day. People could tell time accurately from this marker.

Another Chinese astronomer, Chang Hêng, invented the seismograph, a device that detects earthquakes, in the second century A.D. His seismograph had eight metal dragons arranged around a pendulum in the center. Each dragon faced a different direction and held a copper ball in its mouth. When an earthquake shook the structure, a ball dropped, making a loud *clang* when it hit the metal surface below. This attracted the attention of an attendant, who could tell the direction of the quake by drawing a line out from the dragon that had dropped the ball.

People thought Chang Hêng was a clever person until one day when a ball dropped but no one felt an earthquake. They made fun of him, saying that his invention was a fake. This went on for a couple of days until a messenger arrived from a province several

*A model of an
eleventh-century
water clock*

A cutaway of a model of the Cheng Hêng
seismoscope, the first earthquake detector

hundred miles to the northwest. This messenger reported that an earthquake had indeed occurred at the time when Chang Hêng's seismograph had reported it. His instrument could detect an earthquake so far away that no one could feel the tremor!

KITES AND BALLOONS

Chinese records sometimes give the name of the general or emperor who first used a new device rather than the name of the person who invented it. For example, the Chinese knew about kites for several centuries B.C. and drew pictures of them in the fourth century B.C. Their records say that a general named Han Hsin was the inventor.

Actually, Han Hsin lived over a hundred years after those pictures of kites were drawn. Instead of inventing the kite, he made the first known military use of it in the third century B.C. An army he was fighting had fortified itself inside a city that Han Hsin's troops could not conquer. He put some of his men to work digging a tunnel under the walls. At the same time he had others fly a kite over the city. By keeping track of the length of string they let out, he could compute the distance that his men would have to dig in order to come up inside the walls of the city instead of on the outside.

This is the first known use of an aerial device in warfare. Later Chinese generals used kites to signal each other during battles. Sometimes they would send aloft a kite containing whistles and other noisemakers to try to divert or frighten enemy forces. This was especially effective at night, when foes had no way to see what was causing the strange sounds up in the sky.

The Chinese experimented with balloons over two thousand years ago. First they emptied eggshells and made them float by heating the air inside. Later they developed hot-air balloons, which

were often shaped like dragons or birds and floated overhead during special celebrations. This was common practice in the East more than fifteen hundred years before the Montgolfier brothers sent up the first hot-air balloon in France in 1783.

Always a practical people, the Chinese concentrated their scientific efforts on developing the technologies they needed to live better lives, produce food, and protect the country against enemies. This led them to develop many practical inventions long before such discoveries were known elsewhere in the world.

Kite flying

9

CHINA'S SCIENTIFIC HERITAGE

Throughout history Westerners have been fascinated by many things that Chinese science and technology produced, such as good roads and great walls, and by ingenious inventions like gunpowder and printing. At the same time, Europeans have tended to ignore the basic ideas on which this scientific work was built, ridiculing such concepts as yin and yang and the natural flow of the Tao.

This attitude has led to divided views in the West about the usefulness of China's scientific efforts. Europeans eagerly adopted the magnetic compass, but they refused to look at nature in terms of fields of force until such scientists as Michael Faraday (1791–1867), James Clerk Maxwell (1831–1879), and Albert Einstein (1879–1955) showed that these concepts explain many things about electricity, light, and gravity. Jesuit missionaries who visited China late in the sixteenth century were fascinated by the detailed Chinese astronomical records. At the same time they rejected the idea of an infinite, empty universe that lay behind the practical astronomy they so admired.

BORROWED IDEAS

The West got some of its scientific discoveries, or ideas for such discoveries, directly from the East. In other cases, similar things were invented or uncovered separately in different parts of the world. In other cases, an East-West connection cannot be established and may or may not have existed.

Two of the three inventions that Sir Francis Bacon said transformed the world—the compass and gunpowder—were borrowed directly from the East. The transmission of the third idea—printing—is questionable. Some scholars think that Gutenberg knew about the use of movable type in the East before he began experimenting with it in Germany.

The East and West seem to have made separate discoveries of the circulation of the blood and of the process of inoculating people against smallpox. Although the Chinese knew about both of these great medical concepts centuries before they were discovered in Europe, there seems to be no connection between the work in the East and that which followed in the West.

Other cases are less clear, involving the borrowing of some ideas and the separate discovery of others. This is true of the work of German philosopher and mathematician Gottfried Wilhelm Leibniz (1646–1716). Leibniz is considered to be the father of the processes that led to modern mathematical logic. He based his work with symbols and logic on his knowledge of China's written language, which uses characters to express complete ideas instead of separate words and letters. Leibniz had obtained samples of Chinese writing through correspondence with a Jesuit missionary who had been in China.

After publishing his work on mathematical logic in 1666, Leibniz went on to develop the base two, or binary, system of arithmetic that is used today by computers. This is the system that uses 01 for one, 10 for two, 11 for three (two plus one), 100 for four, 101 for five (four plus one), and so on. Leibniz published his work on the binary system late in the seventeenth century and sent a copy of it to the Jesuit missionary with whom he had been corresponding.

To Leibniz's surprise the missionary sent back a set of *I Ching* hexagrams that had been arranged into a specific order by an eleventh-century Chinese scholar named Shao Yung. The priest pointed out that if the unbroken yang lines represent 1 and the broken yin lines 0, Shao Yung's arrangement of the ancient *I Ching* symbols is a mirror image of Leibniz's binary system from 1 to 64!

Had Leibniz seen this eleventh-century arrangement of the *I Ching* earlier? If so, did it inspire the idea for the binary system? We can never know for sure, but most scholars do not think so. Instead, they see this as a case of two people separated by twelve thousand miles of space and six and a half centuries of time arriving at similar ideas entirely on their own while working with systems of symbols and numbers that were familiar to them.

MISGUIDED EFFORTS

The exchange of ideas between East and West has produced a great deal of misinformation as well as useful data. The Jesuit missionaries who arrived in Beijing late in the sixteenth century were the first Europeans to take an interest in Chinese science. From the beginning they sought to correct the Eastern view that everyting is made up of five elements: fire, earth, metal, water, and wood. In place of this idea they taught the Greek concept that all things are composed of four elements: earth, air, fire, and water. The Jesuits could not know that the ideas they were teaching would be abandoned by Western science within a century.

The Jesuits also tried to convince the Chinese to forget about their idea of an infinite, empty universe. Instead, they taught the ancient Greek idea that the earth is at the center of the cosmos, surrounded by spheres that control the movements of the sun, moon, and planets. Again, these missionaries did not know that the ideas they were teaching were out of date. In fact, this concept was already being replaced by new theories formulated by Nicolaus Copernicus (1473–1543), Galileo Galilei (1564–1642), and others whose views of the universe were much closer to Chinese concepts than they were to the teachings of the Jesuits.

ASTRONOMICAL RECORDS

China's astronomy was far ahead of anything being done in Europe for many centuries. When modern researchers want to know what was happening in the skies between 500 B.C. and A.D. 1000 (when Moslem records begin), they look at the list of events compiled by the stargazers of ancient China. There they find accounts of eclipses, comets, and special happenings such as the supernova explosion of 1054.

Modern astronomical findings have shown that the Chinese records are correct. An example of this is the Chinese account of the "guest star" that flared up around 1300 B.C. A nova such as this generally creates the phenomenon known today as a radio-star. A radio-star is a source of radio signals coming from the remains of a star too dim to be seen with even the most powerful telescope.

Modern astronomers read the Chinese records that say a guest star appeared briefly in the vicinity of Antares around 1300 B.C. and focused their receivers on that spot in the sky. They picked up faint radio signals coming from an invisible source where the explosion had taken place over three thousand years ago.

ENERGY AND MATTER

Ancient Chinese thinking about the nature of the universe parallels modern scientific theories in ways that no one could have foreseen a century ago, much less back when the Jesuit missionaries and others were attempting to change the Chinese point of view.

85

When modern science began developing in Europe, it concentrated on the solid parts of atoms and molecules that make up all matter, paying little attention to the forces that hold these particles together.

As long as they thought in this way, Western researchers viewed the Chinese idea of yin and yang as a quaint curiosity unworthy of further attention. They had the same attitude toward the Chinese belief that energy, and the fields of force it creates, is the basic building material of the universe instead of matter, as Western physicists believed.

The work of Faraday and Maxwell with electromagnetic fields, including light, raised many unanswered questions about this Western view. Further discoveries by Einstein and others led to the development of modern nuclear physics and the release of the tremendous forces bound up inside atoms. These discoveries showed that the older Western view could no longer be accepted.

As a result, modern scientists now look at the universe in terms of forces instead of tiny particles of matter. These forces include those found within atoms as well as those that control the orbits of planets in outer space. Modern science, using experimental techniques, has independently arrived at findings similar to those that China's ancient scholars discovered through intuitive methods that used yin and yang.

The fact that modern physics is reaching conclusions similar to their own views would not have surprised the people of ancient China. For centuries they considered their own ideas superior to those of anyone else, so they would have expected others to agree with them eventually.

A SHIFTING BALANCE

For over two thousand years, from the fifth century B.C. to the fifteenth century A.D., China's science and technology was superior to what could be found anywhere else in the world. Then, after two thousand years, the situation changed. Within a few hundred years the West surged far ahead of the East. Why did this happen?

First, technological progress in China has stood still in recent centuries. Their philosophy has stressed ethics over scientific investigation and has said that sages are more important than scientists.

Second, the Chinese refused to have anything to do with ideas that came from other countries; they considered people outside their frontiers to be barbarians.

Finally, people in China became suspicious of anything new and different, even when it originated within China. They were comfortable with what they had and were unwilling to change their ideas or their way of life.

The result was that China clung to old ideas long after they were outdated. Because of this, they missed out on the profound changes that led to the Industrial Revolution in the West, along with the great increase in scientific knowledge that accompanied this major change.

Before Westerners become too smug, however, they might remember that the past two hundred years is a short time compared with the two thousand years during which China led the world in science and technology. Many wonderful things that the Chinese developed during that productive period are still in use throughout the world. The processes that made this book possible (ink, paper, and printing) had their beginnings in ancient China. So do the kites that people fly each spring, the wheelbarrows that gardeners use, and Fourth of July fireworks.

For that matter, the next time the National Aeronautics and Space Administration sends a satellite into orbit, remember that it rides aloft on a rocket—one of many modern technologies based on ideas developed by the people who settled in the great river valleys of China over five thousand years ago.

GLOSSARY

Abacus—A counting frame used in the East since ancient times. The frame has beads strung on crosswires; movement of these allows the operator to rapidly add and subtract numbers and perform other mathematical calculations.

Acupuncture—A form of Eastern medicine used since ancient times involving sticking needles into certain nerve centers (called acupuncture points) around the body to relieve pain or effect cures.

Alchemist—An ancient researcher who used magical means—no longer approved by science—to discover humankind's relationships to nature. Most alchemists believed they could change base metals into gold or extend human life.

Alloy—A mixture of two or more metals that yields a product that is stronger or has other qualities that are different from the metals used to produce it.

Declination—The angle between the direction shown on a compass (magnetic north and south) and that of the actual poles (true north and south.)

Elixir of life—A magical potion sought by alchemists to extend life or to increase feelings of youthfulness.

Gnomon—A vertical pole used to measure the angle of the sun by the shadow it casts.

Guest star—The Chinese name for novas and supernovas, which flare up and burn brightly for a brief time before disappearing from the sight of the naked eye.

Kang—A benchlike structure inside a Chinese house used as a combination table and bed. Heat is often piped in under it from a fire outside, so the kang also provides heat for the house.

Li—A unit of Chinese measurement equal to approximately one-third of a mile.

Millet—A grain grown by the Chinese as a source of food since ancient times.

Movable type—Small blocks of metal, wood, or clay with letters, words, or other characters on them, used for printing. Such blocks can be moved around in the printing form or removed and reused later.

Moxa (also called moxibustion)—An ancient Chinese medical technique in which a heated cone was held close to an acupuncture point to relieve illness or pain.

Tao—In Chinese philosophy, the "way" or "path" that individuals and society as a whole should follow to achieve harmony and to have a comfortable, productive life.

Yin and yang—Two basic forces of the universe that control events and express in people's lives. The yang represents the warm, dry, active things and the masculine, intellectual side of individuals. The yin is the cold, wet, passive side of things and the feminine, intuitive qualities of individuals.

FOR FURTHER READING

Clayre, Alasdair. *The Heart of the Dragon*. Boston: Houghton Mifflin, 1985. Contains an excellent chapter on Chinese science, technology, and medicine, including a discussion of the reasons for China's decline in these areas.

Gernet, Jaques. *A History of Chinese Civilization*. Cambridge: Cambridge University Press, 1982. A history of China from earliest times to the present.

Hay, John. *Ancient China*. New York: Henry Z. Walck, 1973. Covers Chinese history and progress from ancient times through the Han Dynasty (200 B.C. to A.D. 200).

McLenighan, Valjean. *Enchantment of the World of China*. Chicago: Children's Press, 1983. Summarizes major accomplishments of each dynasty from prehistoric times to the modern era.

Needham, Joseph. *Science and Civilization in China*. Cambridge: Cambridge University Press. Seven volumes have been projected;

five have been completed by the mid-1980s. The most definitive work on science in ancient China. A good reference.

Ross, Frank Jr. *Oracle Bones, Stars, and Wheelbarrows*. Boston: Houghton Mifflin, 1982. An excellent account of ancient Chinese science and technology, told in an entertaining style for young people.

Walker, Richard. *Ancient China*. New York: Franklin Watts, 1969. Traces Chinese life from prehistoric times through the Han Dynasty, with notes on more recent times.

Walsh, Richard. *Adventures and Discoveries of Marco Polo*. New York: Random House, 1953. An account of Marco Polo's trip to China in the thirteenth century. This book for young people is based on actual words written by the great traveler.

INDEX

ABOUT THE AUTHOR

George Beshore has written about scientific and environmental subjects for newspapers, magazines, and the federal government for over twenty-five years. He is now a fulltime free-lance writer. Mr. Beshore lives in Alexandria, Virginia.